WRITTEN AND ILLUSTRATED BY DARKO NO. 52

SANDWICH

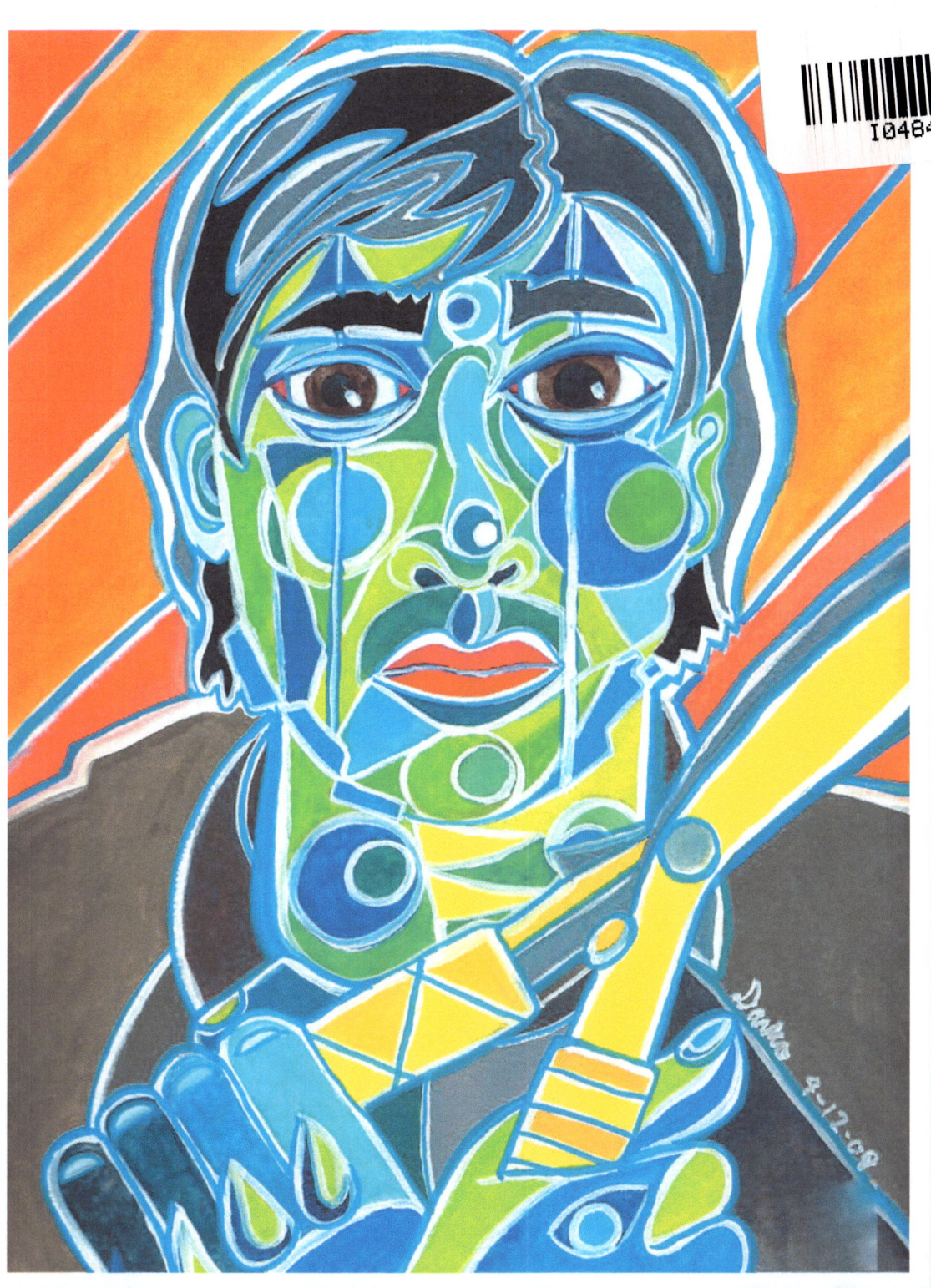

Special thanks for editing to Tom Obee

This book was printed in the United States of America.

To order additional copies of this book, contact:
Xlibris Corporation
1-888-795-4274
www.Xlibris.com
Orders@Xlibris.com

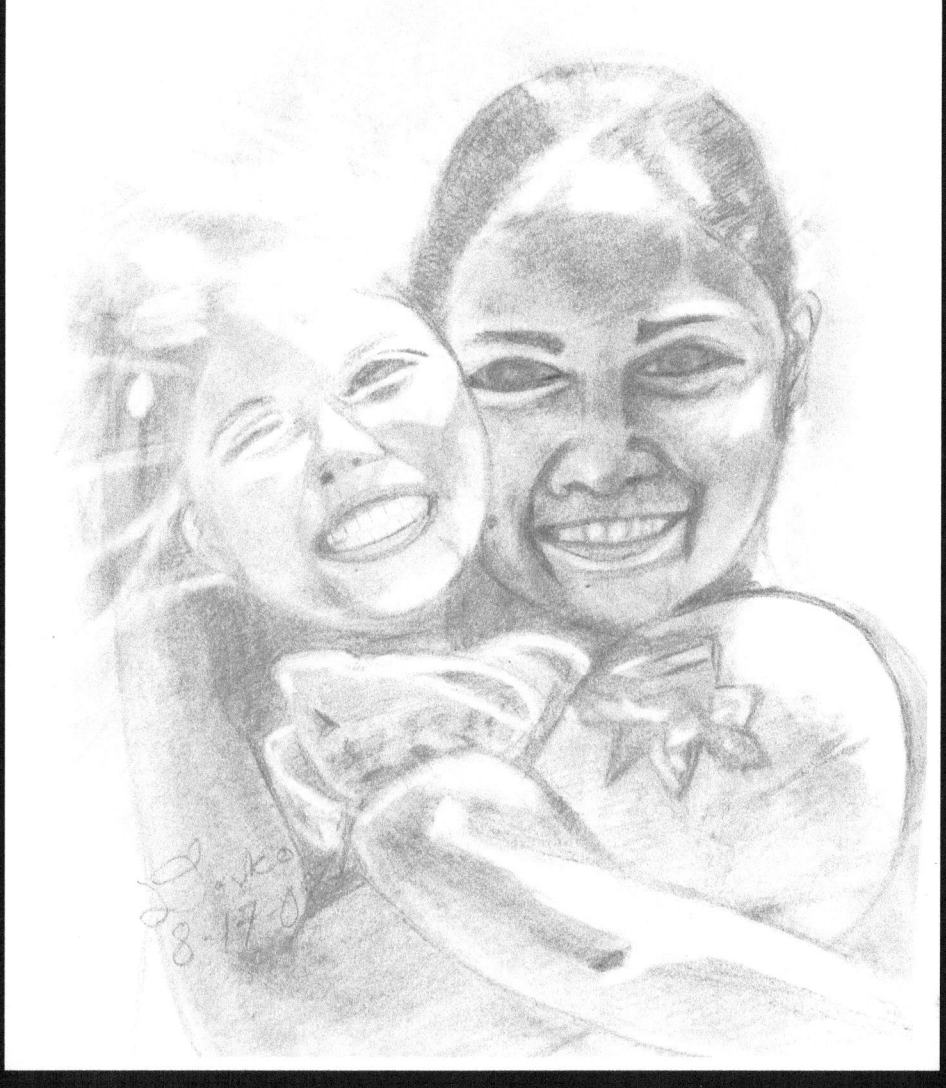

TO MY EMILINE,
THE LOVE OF MY LIFE.

My Best Friend

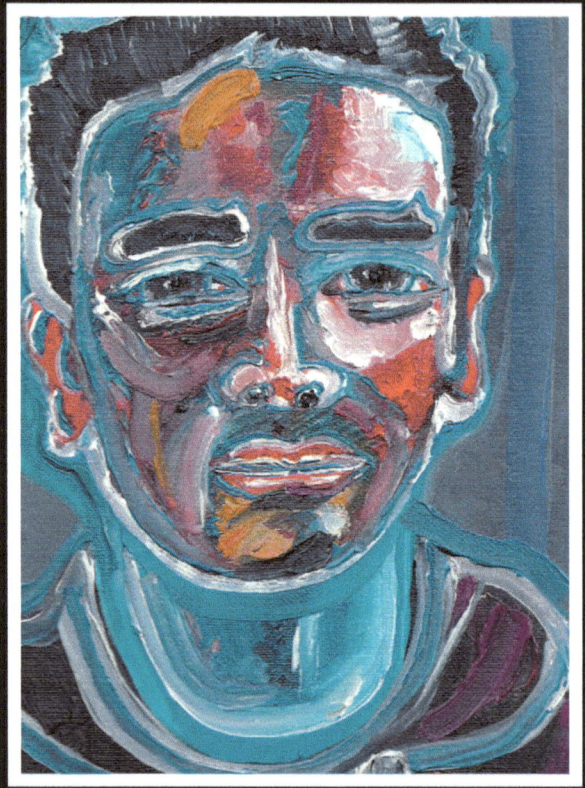

On an eerie, brisk, cold winter morning, I awoke from a devil's nightmare, wanting to escape the slumber to avoid the Hell I lived in. I'm here to see my good loving friend Dim Rodas.

I'm seated in this black room illuminated with five windows, one on my left, and four on my right. Draped with sultry crushed purple velvet, the windows are long and thin. Aligned with the window is a wooden frame. The drapes cut off half of the dark, violent, naked world that lies beyond the black walls. An orange luminous beam break the skyline cascading through the velvet, causing me to reminisce of tangerine oranges my friend's momma would peel for him when he was a child. Dim once told me how he remembered eating them as if he could still

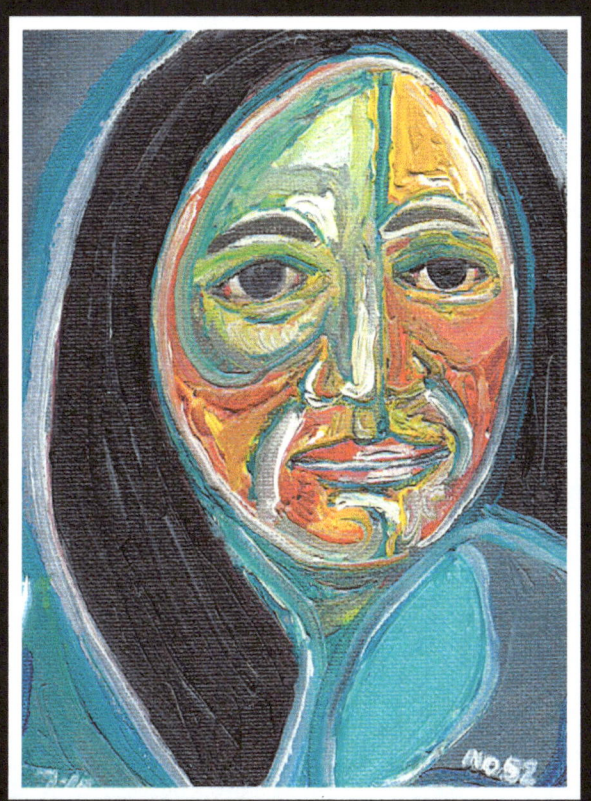

taste the bitterness against the bumps in his mouth. Dim's momma would quickly place the tangerine slices on the short wooden table that had been beaten up due to age. The slices were placed right next to syringes that were full of heroin. With the sense of guilt still in Dim's mind, he held on to the dark memories. His momma asked him if the tangerines tasted sweet. "Yes, Momma, they're as sweet as the dew of a perfect wedge on a ripe honeydew melon." He told that white lie just so he didn't upset her. But the thing about lying is you do that to protect something, usually something that you hold dear to your heart. I don't understand why he tried to protect her; why did he lie to himself? I wondered to myself, as I unwrapped a foiled piece of Pink Devil Chewing Gum. I began to chew the gum; it helped clear my mind of all impressions.

His momma was a very nice woman, almost so nice that it was detrimental to Dim. Sometimes having a red cotton handkerchief wrapped around her head, she had one of those images about her that you could see on a box of pancake batter mix. What a woman, I tell myself; I just felt sorry for her. Looking at his momma you see the origin of Dim.

Dim is such an unusual name. He told me that he got the name on the day he was born. On that day there was a lightning storm. All the electricity was out; his dad lit the rooms with white soft candles. The sky cried tears as his momma pushed him out in the lowly lit room of the house. With the lights flickering, the baby was born into the Dim glow of the room.

My best friend, Dim, had a funny looking hair cut; it was jet black and shaved on the sides. He stood short, but he was quite tall if you were looking at him squinting with one eye; peeking at him cockeyed with nothing there around him. Dim was fragile-looking but really was strong at heart.

He saw that trusting me was easy, as he opened up to me. One of the chapters of his life he didn't talk much about with just anybody was his dad. Always wearing expensive clothes and sporting a brownish orange beard, his dad talked with a mean raspy voice, the one that slashed out through the rooms. When he yelled, it sounded like an old wood four by four with splinters getting twisted until all the fibers snapped into two. Dad's whispers hissed of a whimpering, ratted-out old blow whistle. His unfriendly voice was one you can point out in a second in a deep thick crowd. He stood like a protruding thumb kissing the great yellow sky.

At the times Dim mentioned his dad it burned inside of my very inner being. I've remembered almost everything about him. He was a Stone Doctor. His dad always carried a revolver with him, was never seen without it. The Stone Doctor was one of the richest ones in the city. Bread ruled his world views and it later consumed him. Fear spawned a nickname for his dad. Dim often called his daddy "the monster."

As Dim ran in circles on a road shaped like a clock that led to nowhere and the sounds of his dirty old blue shoes pounded the pavement, echoes rippled into my imagination: the stories of horror that Dim once told me of the beatings he had faced under the hands of the monster. Dim and his momma always tried to escape the cold stone fists of the monster by running to the neighbor's car parked in the backyard. The car was an unlocked, rusted-out brown station wagon. They lied in the back of the car scared only to be under the bright stars that Dim was born under. The yellow dots blanketing the aquamarine sky protected them from the pain, making them feel safe as they prayed to Jehovah and clasped their hands close together, writing letters in

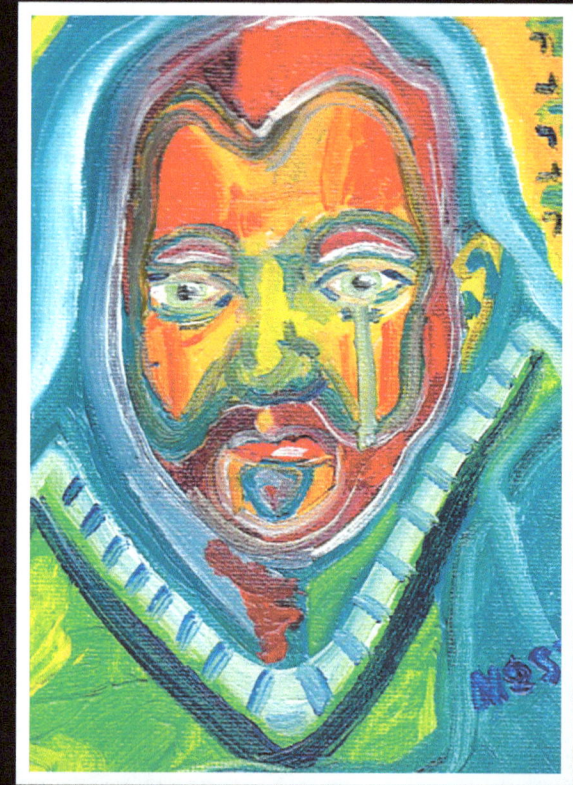

their mind for help, speaking the sentences under their scratchy cold breath.

But often there were times that Dim and his momma couldn't run away from the monster. The consequences were sharp and intense, as he suffered by the monster's stone cold fists, and his mouth, the entrance to Hell. His hands had Dim's blueprint on them. The monster often terrorized his momma, but he never touched her, he had mercy on her. Dim was the focus of his wrath; many times he was almost beaten to death. Why did the monster hate Dim so much? My best friend had such innocence about him. I could never comprehend at all why anyone would hurt him. To this day I feel so awful about the horror Dim went through. His momma never called for help; the shame and the guilt of the beatings that Dim took at the hands of the monster consumed her. I shed tears for him in despair. His momma never called for help. Why? She must have been trapped in the tower with an invisible fence made of terror. Maybe it was because of the knowledge of the monster's revolver.

I look out the window waiting for Dim, and I see the great winter brooding, my most loved time of the season. Every Christmas I reminisce upon my very own years of my boyhood. My momma spoiled me so much that it made me feel a colorless high. She bought me all I wanted and I felt like a prince in a palace on a snowy day. All the toys I could want she would pay for. The white snowflakes floated in the cool hard air drifting forward and backward as it kissed the brown dirt. Dozing off I cannot remember the bad.

One day the beatings ended, Dim told me. He came home early from school on his birthday, after he went to the toy store with his momma. It was a dream to Dim, one that caused him to feel blinded and deaf. He picked out a red toy motorcycle for his birthday. He was playing with the new toy, making tracks on the kitchen table as momma was cooking dinner. The sounds of the toy, mixed with that of the children in the other apartments. The hard rubber wheel ran across the table. As it shuffled across the dining room, it caused beautiful music as of an orchestra that was never heard before. As Dim played the sounds of fake booming engine of the toy, momma was cutting the carrots for the vegetable soup that she was making. Dim looked over, and saw the knife created dents in the wood of the old beaten-up cutting board. He could hear the eggs frying in the pan the seeds from a chicken sizzling and biting the warm air throughout the smoky kitchen. The chopping sounds and the boom of the toy generated a symphony throughout the whole complex.

Abruptly the door slammed open. BOOM! The monster was home, the birthday had come to a sudden end. The monster beat Dim, pummeling and whipping the boy that was his own seed. Momma came rushing to stop the monster. As she and daddy became twisted into each other, they struggled for the control of the revolver from his pocket that the monster had been so faithful to. POP! Silence rang throughout the compound. Momma was bleeding... She was bleeding heavily. Dim told me he could hear death enter the room before losing his hearing. I don't remember too much of what Dim said after this, I just don't. But a few days later after Dim's mommy was taken to the hospital, she died. His dad was immediately charged and convicted of murder.

The last I heard of Dim's dad, he was in prison, he owed six hundred sixty nine stamps. What I heard was the stamps were used for legal tender in the prison. He owed all this in gambling debts. The people he owed shanked him in the stomach and he bled out, an excruciating death, just as Dim's momma did.

Dim received a letter from his dad two weeks after the monster's death. It was a possible psychological explanation for the beatings Dim received, but he never finished the letter, nor did he keep it.

Pop! Pop... pop... pop! The sounds of a white dove flying in the blue heavens hitting the pane of the stained glass window rings throughout the room I sit in. It cracks the window, leaving a mist of blood on the bits of the crystals. I get up and move to view the window to see if the dove is still alive. I only see that I can't find the dove. The reflections in the glass leave my very own image cut up into many pieces. It leaves me as once before when I sporadically pondered something opening up my soul and just pouring love into my heart. My heart lacks this emotion. I pray to Jehovah to kindly find my love. At many times I am convinced that I've possibly lost my soul somewhere. Truth says that I indeed have lost it. Please, I wonder if I could just have it back, if I could be just so lucky. I recollect life flashing before me. I notice a ruler in heavenly paradise. Standing in my sights a halo shines; blinding me to my very own identity. The nimbus speaks, uttering the voice that is indescribable to my soft fleshy ears. Like most dreams I don't remember what was said. Just in hearing the rushing cry of water running down my face, I'm able to realize that I was in the presence of actual holiness.

In this dark lit room with the corners of my elbows slightly bent looking like french bread, my body drooped over, sitting before Dim Rodas. Two of my fists softly press up against my supple cheeks. Pain and sorrow stir in my head. Dim Rodas' devitalized body that has perished, is set, deposited in a wooden box made of simple white pine, decorated very plainly.

I look down at my bare wrists, as I gnaw on my Pink Devil Chewing Gum. I have sizable regrets, never having a gold Pelican wrist watch. Just being somebody noteworthy was something I wanted all my life. If someone asked me the time of day, I could look down at my beautiful time keeper and say it's 4:25 p.m., but now I know I'll never have that chance.

A prank phone call came to my mind. It rewound all my memories and I saw how I took my last breath as I sat in the chair dead. That last fix scratching the internal itch that ran through my veins ultimately killed me. A fiend freak, a junkie, that is what I am. I station myself as a slave to my addiction, Heroin.

As I stand alone in this room with my body before me, I am gone, no more. Such intensely rooted sadness runs through the purple threads in my body.

My momma once told me that you're born into the world with someone there but you die alone. I feel so lonely, not a soul there for me, but I do have myself. I am my best friend, Dim Rodas.

THE END

NEVER FORSAKE MYSELF

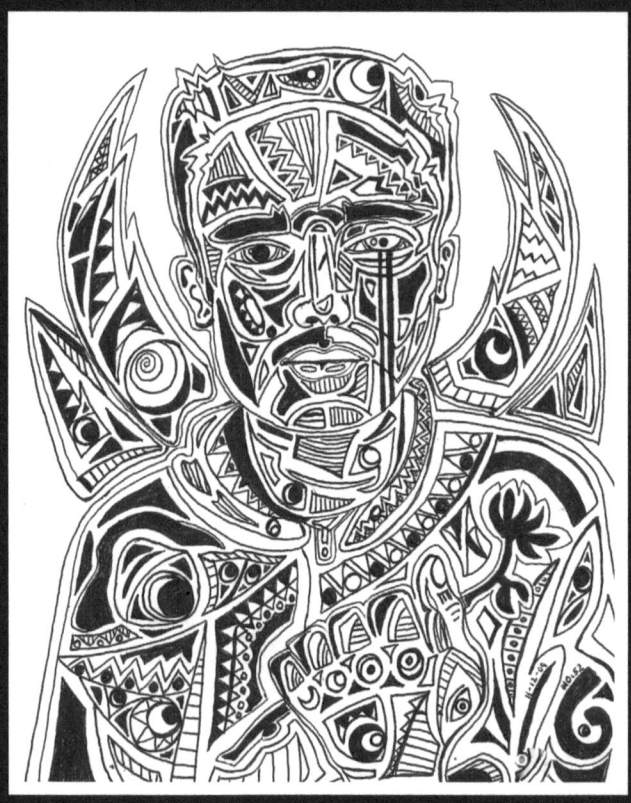

On the morning the drizzle turned to snow showers, I was kneeling beside a young woman on her death bed. As I stood there I knew God had cursed me with a gift that deceived me. I am hated by one man, myself, which is by far the greatest number. My freakish, bizarre ability to read people's minds has left me to care about no soul but my very own. I don't want the contrasting problems to reside within me. I have too many problems of my own.

Radiant images are projecting in my mind. I am able to read feelings and thoughts. Many think I'm gifted from God, but there are also people that think I'm crazy. Hating the gift is to despise myself, which I do.

The end of the world is near, you hear the jibber jabber of the people of the earth. I welcome it with all open arms. End my pain, my affliction, my loneliness. In the loneliness I drive myself to nowhere, away from home. I recognize this as human garbage, which I and our society has incubated. The women and the children of the world leave me so bitter, as mankind has left me so very disgusted by the way and the means of living my own life.

I will not end this life of mine by slaying myself simply because of this. There is something that is eternally inside of me, a speck of light I've seen since the very beginning of my life. This light gives me a hope... this hope that I was loved with an unconditional attachment to something warmly devoted to me ... forever.

I was drawn to this young woman as she called me through her thoughts. She spoke words that twirled ideas of the world to me. This great beam that I followed across the city led me to her bedside. A blazing fire of light extended itself to me, asking me to follow it. It was there, I was led to a young woman who was dying. She was gravely sick from a disease that the world had given her. I was told she was speechless and silent with the inability to hear, not being able to discern the babel in which she lived.

I feel this was the preamble to the conclusion to my existence. I only hope that it's fallacious and unfounded. Although I have no conclusion, roaming and dawdling within my faculties, I only hoped this woman had something to offer me: A solution for some higher quality of manner for me.

I could see her stare at me with such love... such love which I can't comprehend with involvement, for I was for not loved at any moment in my life. As a baby, I was abandoned by my parents from the very beginning of my existence.

There reflecting in my mind, an angel... a messenger of God cast down to the ruins of the earth where he met a young woman. A mortal... the messenger that he fell in love with. It was then he became a fallen angel, tumbling down to the earth. She displayed a deepest love conceivable to this person, who was a saint as well.

After the hour stood still, a divine being was born. There was no abomination, just love. I despise many things in life, but I am able to keep myself from hating this. This was simply sublime, a multi-color of psychedelic brilliance striking me with such kindness. The presence of Jehovah was upon me.

As I kneel on both knees I then am told by this woman... she is my mother. My mom... the one who gave birth to me. I am disturbingly dumbfounded and astonished that I now have an origin... a beginning. This woman is no longer uncomfortable but lies dying. Not audible and also unable to speak, she is intoxicated by all of her senses. I'm finding love of my fortunes in life, the substantial gifts of my own being. Learning to adore her, as my father had loved her, is a great gift to me. Finally I have found something that was missing all my life... my mom and me.

The dawning of the day turned to the crow of the night. My mom died in my arms as she turned into a cherub. Bent like a weeping tree mourning the young love, I see in my mom the love she had for me. I learned to forgive my despair. My gifts of insanity no longer need to be practiced. Standing alone, I learned to love and laugh. I'm going home, not to a building or a place... but a state of mind. From then on, I learned to never forsake myself.

THE END

MUSTARD. MOUNTAIN. MAN.

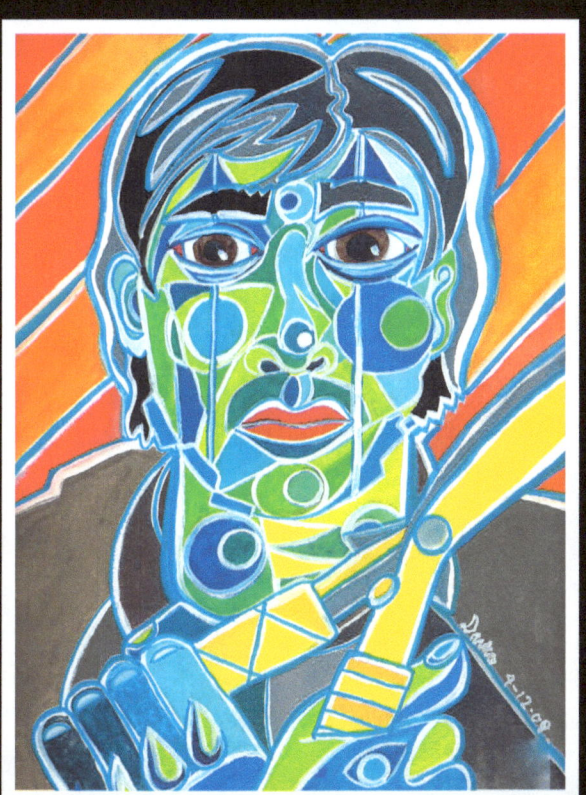

Long ago in Japan there was an old farmer named Mustard Fuji that had a very beautiful daughter Kokorosan. Mustard Man the farmer was ostracized by the village as he would hear voices every so often. The village people thought of him as crazy. Being one of the only Christians in the village did not help him. There was a church in the middle of the village although the community was predominantly Buddhist.

One day as Mustard Man was working on his farm he was approached

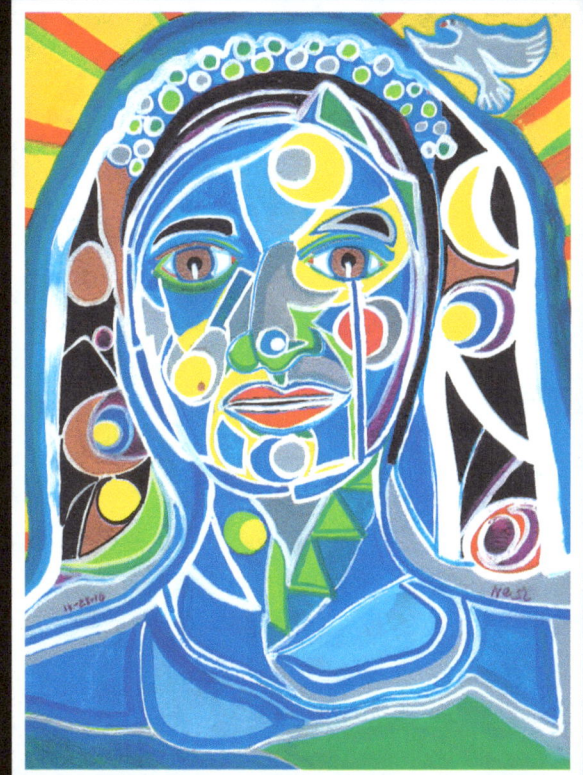

by an odd and mysterious looking man with a very black and gray curly beard. The man gave Mustard Man a pair of shiny golden shears. As he was very pleased with them the gift was accepted. He bowed to him, then thanked the stranger. The farmer continued working. After a morning's work Mustard Man went off to drink green tea at his neighbor Raitosan's house as he did every Sunday morning to escape his loneliness on the weekends. His wife had died many years ago leaving him only a loving daughter Kokorosan.

After drinking his tea and going home there was a knock on his door. Mustard Man slid open the rice paper door and found the strange man who had given him the golden shears.

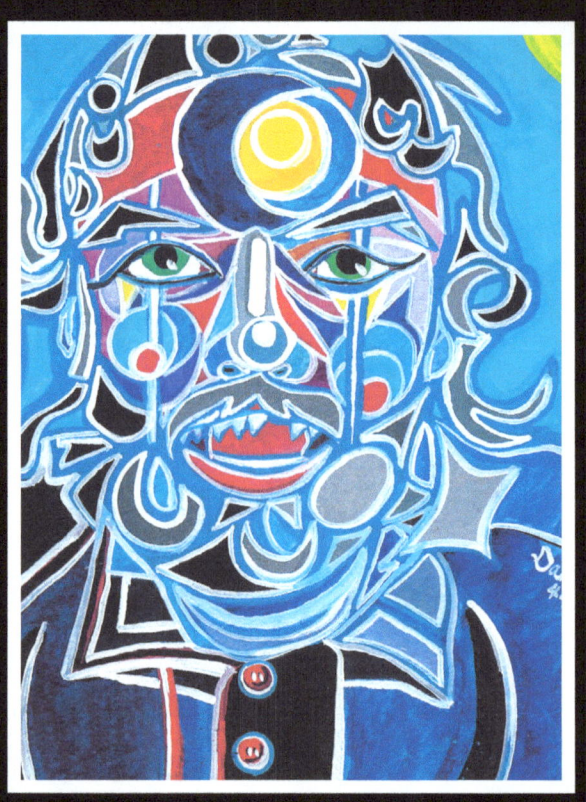

"Dun. Dun. Dun. I ask for your daughter's hand in marriage. Dun. Dun. Dun." the strange man said.

"Why do you come here? Do you want the golden shears back?"Mustard Man asked.

The strange man said "Dun. Dun. Dun. No, I want to marry your beautiful daughter. Dun. Dun. Dun."

"I'm sorry my daughter is engaged to be married to a merchant named Jibunsan from another village. They will marry soon," said Mustard Man. Then the mysterious man left in a huff.

The next morning Raitosan came over to look at Mustard Man's flowers, as on the previous day he had asked how they were doing. Mustard Man was pruning his flowers with his new golden shears.

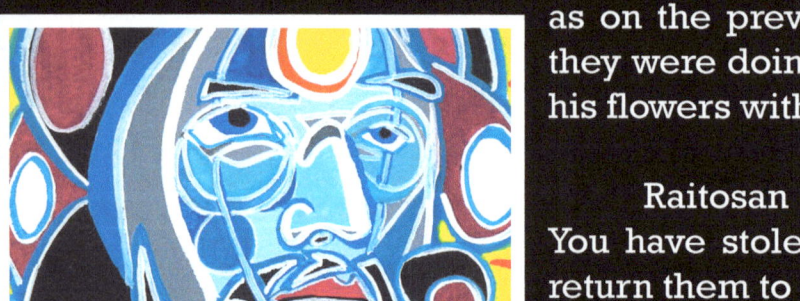

Raitosan said, "Those are my shears. You have stolen my golden shears. Please return them to me immediately! "

Mustard Man exclaimed, "I received these from a strange man... uh...."

Mustard Man stopped mid-sentence and decided to just give the golden shears to Raitosan. After all he thought, how many golden shears exist? They must have been his so he returned them. That was the Christian thing to do, he thought to himself.

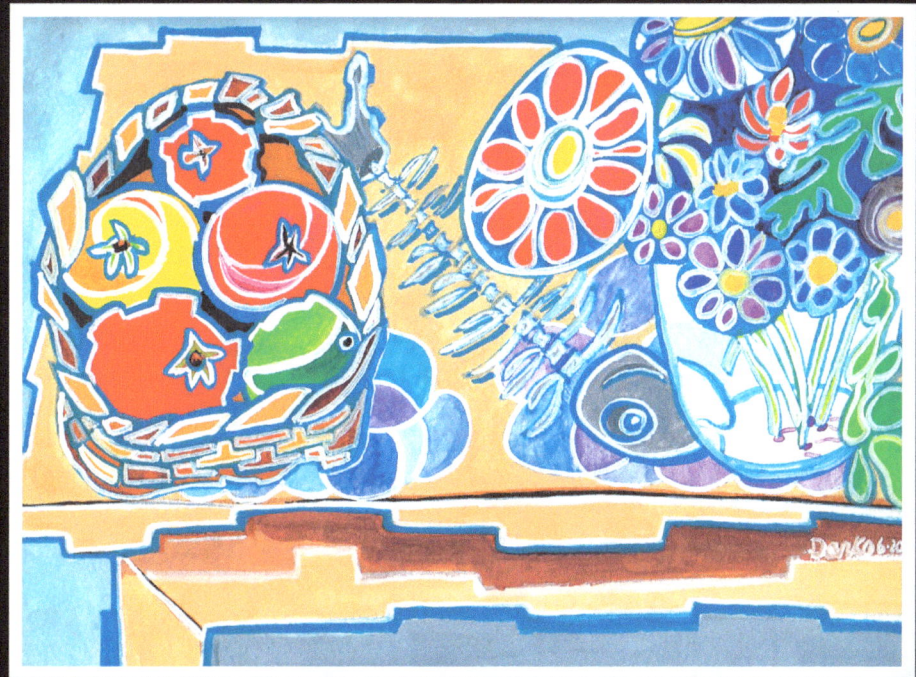

The neighbor was very sad but left in peace. The next day Mustard Man was watering his flowers. And the strange man showed up again. Once again he said, "Dun. Dun. Dun. I would like to marry your daughter. Dun. Dun. Dun."

Mustard Man with frustration said, "I'm sorry but I will not allow you to marry her."

"Dun. Dun. Dun. So then it shall be, return my shears or I shall kill you by sundown next Sunday! Dun. Dun. Dun."

"I have not any shears, I gave them away," Mustard Man said sadly.

"Dun. Dun. Dun. Then I have nothing more to say, Dun. Dun. Dun," replied the strange man as he grumbled and stormed off.

Mustard Man was a man of peace; he could not fight or kill the stranger. The next morning he decided to plea to the emperor.

"Please, my great emperor, a man has threatened my life. He has given me a pair of golden shears to marry my daughter, only I found out that they were stolen from my neighbor's farm. Not having the shears now as I have returned them to their rightful owner, I have no shears to give to the man who is to kill me. He will kill me by sundown on Sunday night. I beg you, emperor, help me!" Mustard Man began weeping.

The emperor had never heard such a thing. Golden shears... marry his daughter? The emperor found this humorous. He asked for a description of the mystery man, as he tilted his head thinking. The emperor had all of his servants search for the stranger in the village to resolve the matter.

After two days had passed, Mustard Man's daughter Kokorosan was married at a wondrous wedding. She then moved away with Jibunsan. Mustard Man had his morning cup of tea and he was summoned by the emperor. He had found the stranger.

"Was this the man that had threatened you?" the emperor asked. There stood the same strange man. He had spun out ebony hair with a long curly beard and sharp teeth.

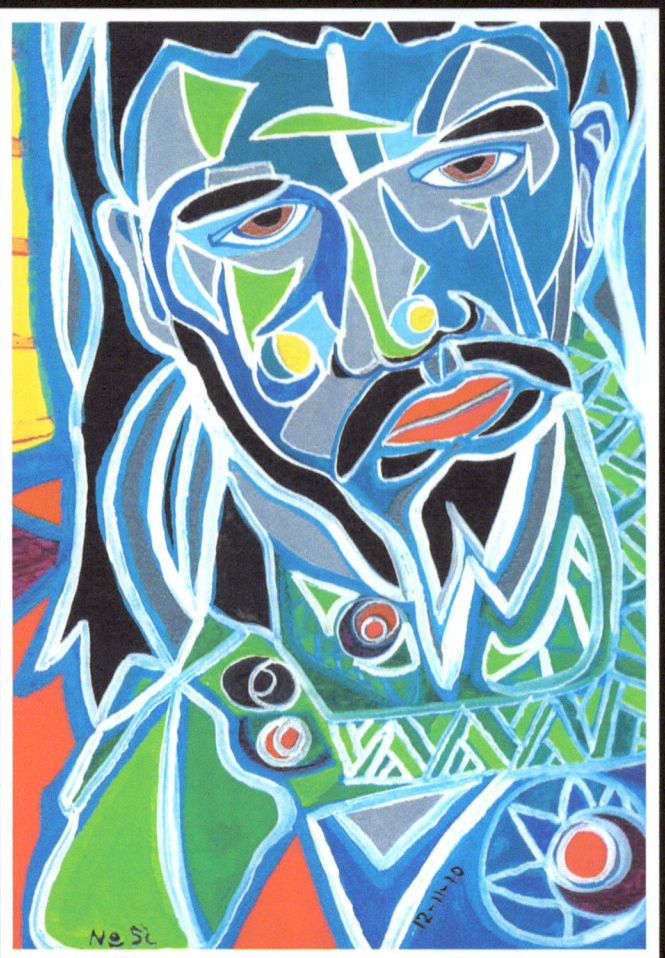

"Yes, yes! That is the man who has threatened to kill me by sundown tonight." replied Mustard Man.

The emperor began to laugh. "This strange man is mute, he cannot hear or speak. How could he have threatened you?"

Mustard Man was embarrassed. He left the palace shaking his head, confused, unsure of what had happened. That night Mustard Man went home scared. He began to think about stealing his neighbor's golden shears to give to the stranger to save his life. Mustard Man after much meditation decided not to steal the golden shears as it was against his religion to do so. He decided to have faith in God as he was home waiting for the stranger to show up. He questioned himself. Was it the voices that he heard in his past? Was the man really a mute? Was the man really out to kill him? Mustard Man began to pray. Then he left early to go to church. In the empty church he knelt down in front of the altar. Suddenly the stranger appeared and stabbed Mustard Man with his sword and left him there to bleed.

The strange man yelled and screamed at the sky "Dun. Da, da. Dun. Dun..........DUN!" as he ran into the sunset.

As the story of Mustard Man's death spread amongst the village the emperor became aware of the true identity of the murderer. His name was Mountain Man. He was a known thief and liar in the village. The emperor was very sad that he was mistaken. He was regretful that he did not believe Mustard Man. The emperor decided to order for Mountain Man to be found and executed at once.

To honor Mustard Fuji, the great emperor had his servants build another church in the village made of pure gold. On top of the church the farmer had died in, the emperor ordered for a mountain to be moved, an act which took a century to complete. Mustard Man was buried there in the church and every so often the mountain would erupt with liquid fire. As the wise-tale says it's because Mustard Fuji is weeping tears of lava from the village in which he had lived. The emperor in tribute to Mustard Man forever named the mountain Mt. Fuji.

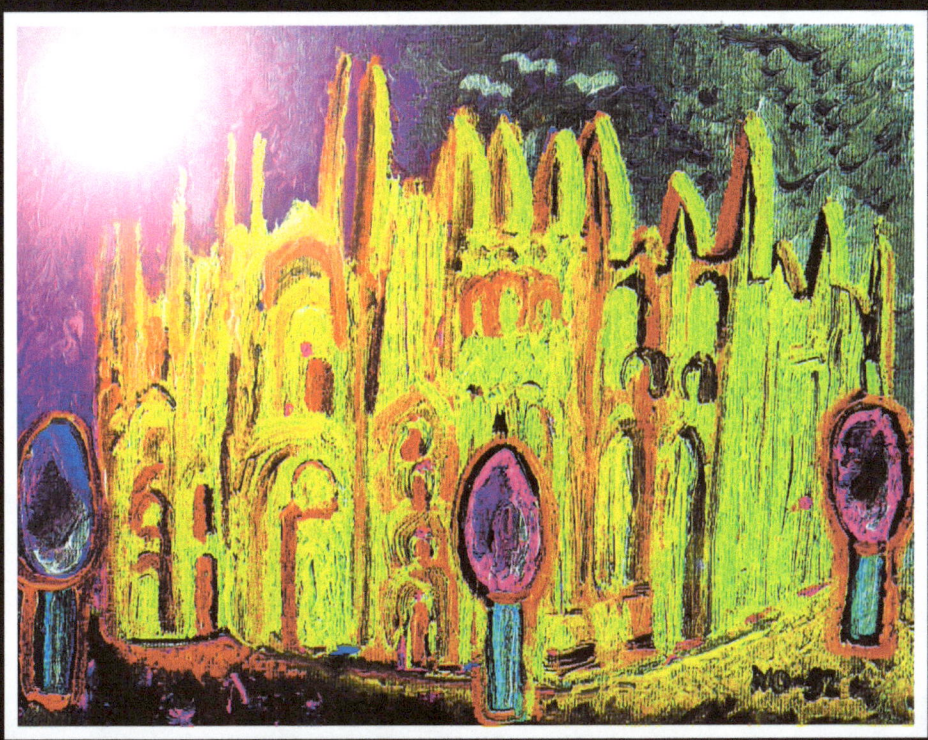

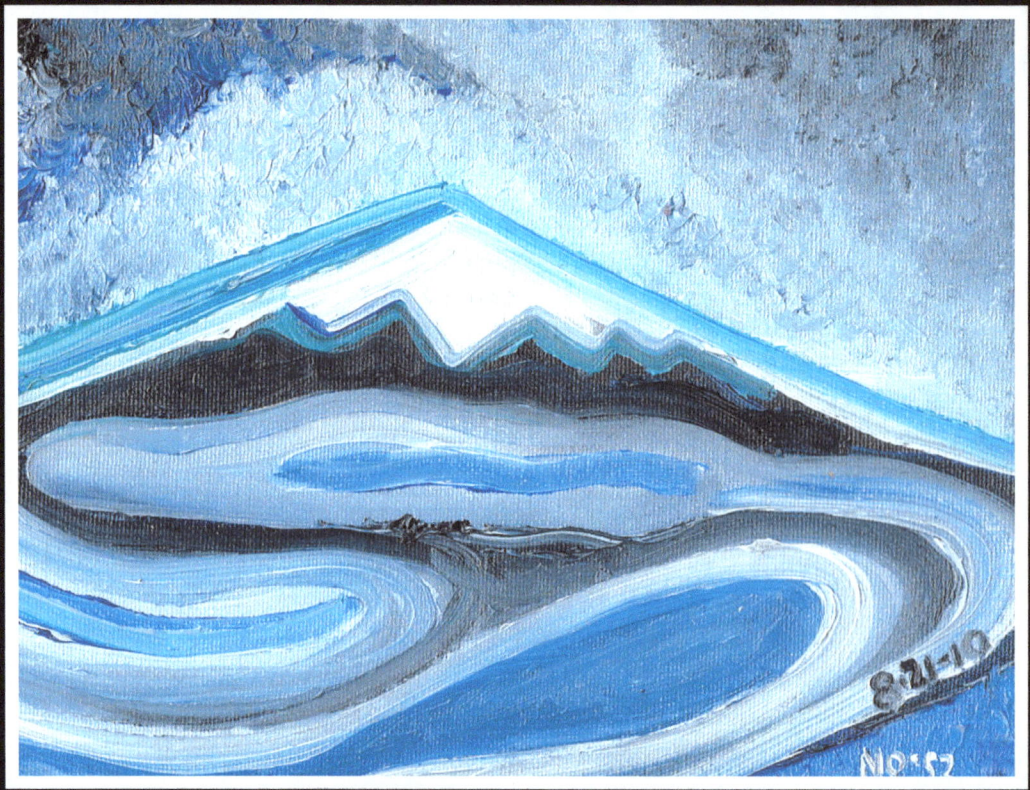

THE END

LOVING THE SUN

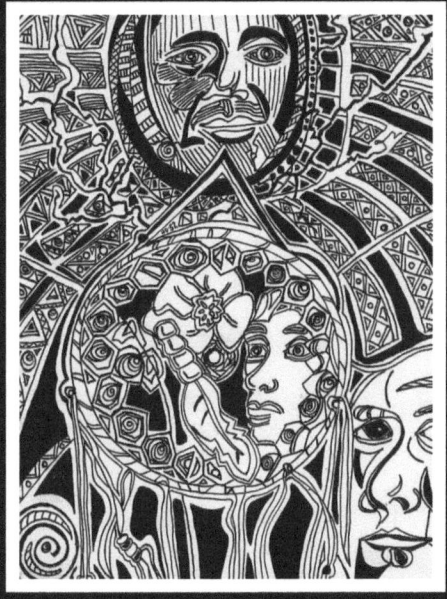

A beautiful princess child adored the great Sun. She bathed in the silky smooth rays of his love. The Sun's streaks beamed and radiated throughout the earth's smoke. The Sun also loved the divine princess and showed it with a soft delicate kiss. But the kiss killed the little star child. Thereafter, the Sun slept every night dreaming of her. But then the princess' memory fell into the hands of incubus, the monster that watched over all nightmares of man. The Sun had fallen into melancholy, and the lights went out, as her absence had left him all alone. Battling for the memory of his love, the Sun set out to defeat the monster. After the Sun and incubus clashed, he rescued her, and brought her back to his sleep. Princess child became reborn for eternity in his dreams. Her mother laid underneath the Sun waiting for her child to come home but she never did. The princess was living in bliss in paradise with the Sun. Eventually she became the moon. They both took turns watching high over the souls of the children, spreading their love over the earth. And that's what happened for loving the Sun.

THE END

An Ebony Tulip

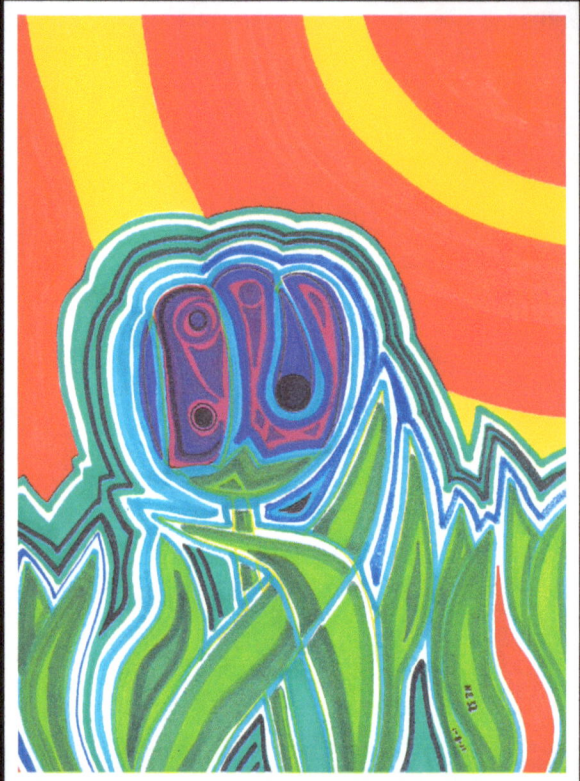

Every mid spring an old man who watched over his flowers, picked the most beautiful one out of his yard. He brought it into his home to display it on his dinner table.

Because of a mistake by the gardener, only two flowers grew this year. The one flower was given two names. The first one, the ebony tulip was named Wine. It yelled and screamed out every morning at the bright impairing morning sun. The beautiful dark Wine color rooted the base for its name.

Glass was the name of the second flower. Because it was crying all night long, the lawn named it Glass. It felt ugly with its weeping petals. Glass was a very soft sensitive flower. That caused Glass to be rejected by all the plants on the lawn. The great Sun and the Moon told young Glass every day that he

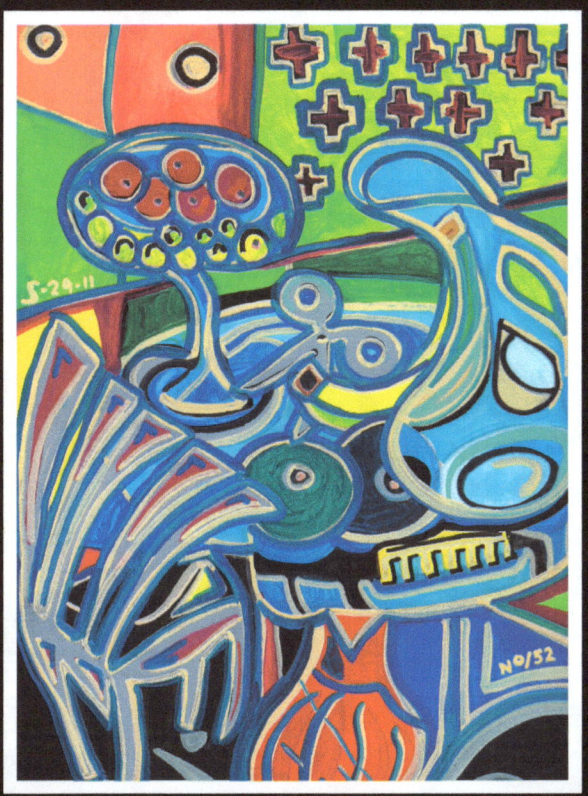

was beautiful. But the baby flower didn't believe the sun or the moon.

Wine, on the other hand, was full of confidence, almost so much that it was arrogant in its beauty. As Wine had attention of the whole lawn, the man of the garden came by to the flower bed to make his pick for the most beautiful flower. He swooped down with his small steel scissors and snapped the stem as he cut his choice the darling little Wine tulip. Glass was so distraught over not being picked. The next morning the sky yawned as it began raining. Rain drops fell and rolled off Glass's petals, which tottered down. As Glass collected up the water droplets, the flower began to wilt and bend. He then knelt down to a suckling water pond that had collected before himself. Glass saw his own reflection in the puddle. Right then he realized he was a mirror image of Wine. Glass was planted in the earthly soil as an ebony tulip.

THE END

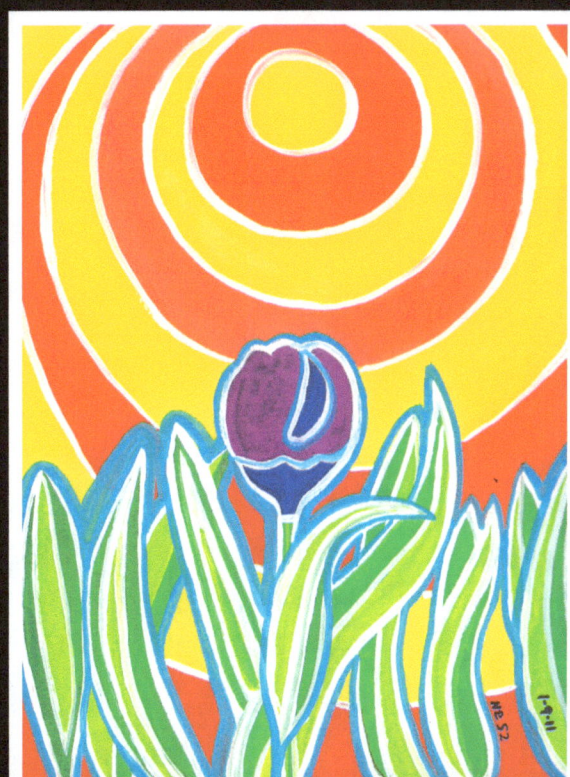

My Art Form Kirilism

Lines/Aura - All items and objects have an azure contour. A blurring aura saturates their external form. All auras radiate away from the subject. This in sum is captured by Kirilism. The effects are not in theory aesthetic, but in reality loyal to their own beauty and elegance.

Shapes/Colors - Circular and round shapes draw positive emotions; angular or pointed shapes attract negative emotions. Colors can hold different emotions with every hue, just like spices can hold a different taste with every kind.

Meaning - When looking at subjects there are emotions we have or want to have or want to express. By using round and angular shapes - and an array of colors- Kirilism professes to convey a feeling that is objective. Beauty is not in all things. Kirilism is a search and a journey to find beauty in the human psyche.

Balance - Life is full of imperfections and flaws. Art portrays this through line, color, and shape. Kirilism shows flaws and is asymmetrical as well as symmetrical. In Kirilism, all elements are created on purpose to create an intentional result. A balance between positive and negative is important. If the subject is negative then most of the ten elements need to show positive traits. This gives the feel of apprehension or wonderment-as opposed to simply happiness or sadness- provoking people to ask questions of life. For instance, a still picture created with Kirilism could be a black cotton ball. The color, size, distance, focus, view, and all other elements with a negative emotion would balance the positive, fluffy subject, which is normally considered white. If the art has constant motion-like movies, it at first needs to be all negative or positive. Then the final segment is to show the opposite emotion, which creates balance. But what's important is to show the objects out of their realm with its emotional elements. A sample of a picture that has motion would be a scene with a woman's back upper/point of view, open/body, out of focus, distance/far, color/light walking down an open alley. Then suddenly pulling out a jagged stone, the camera would show abruptly a frontal view point, as she breaks the glass window. That would create balance in Kirilism.

Distance - To show outer and inner insight, distance is shown in Kirilism. All for aesthetic reasons. Same angle, different distance.

- and + chart

1) shape	angle	round
2) color	dark	light
3) size	big	small
4) distance	close	far
5) focus	in	out
6) object open/closed	closed	open
7) texture	hard	soft
8) showing front/back	front	back
9) POV down/up	down	up
10) object vertical/horizontal	vertical	horizontal
11) subject matter	-	+

Examples of Kirilism: See pictures of *Wine, Raitosan, Mom, Church, Kokorosan, Loving the Sun,* and *Table.*

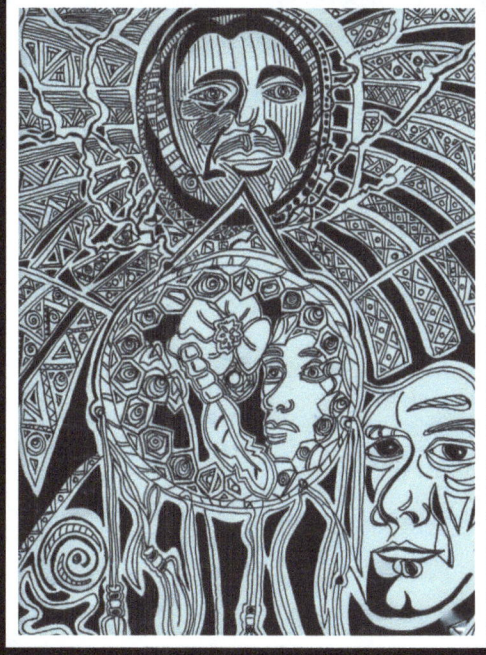
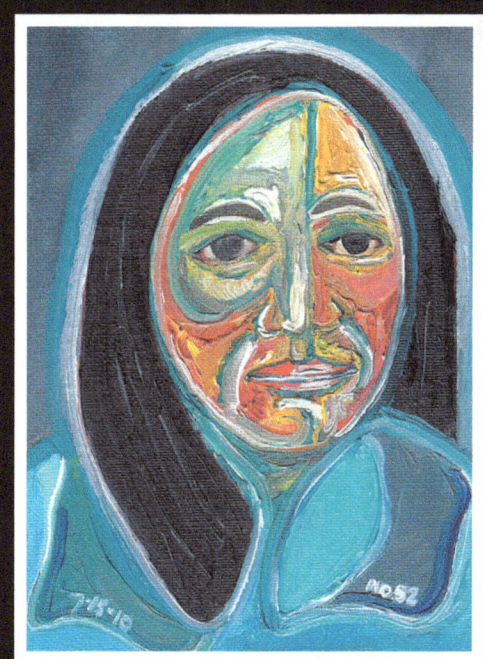

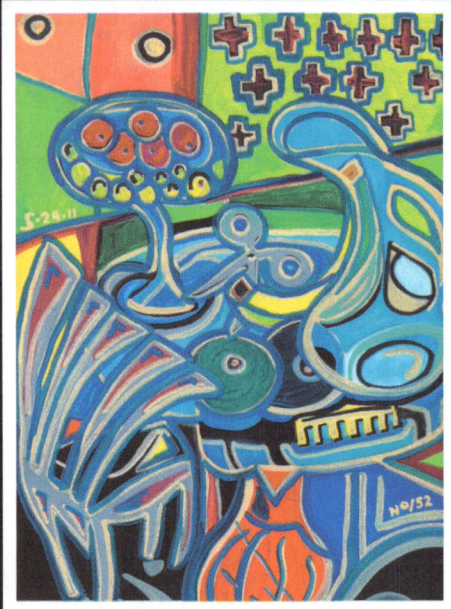
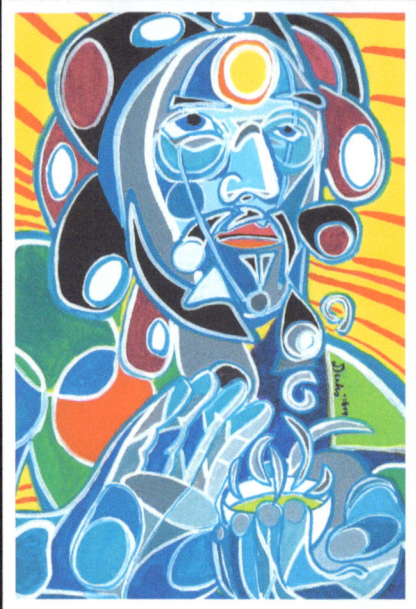
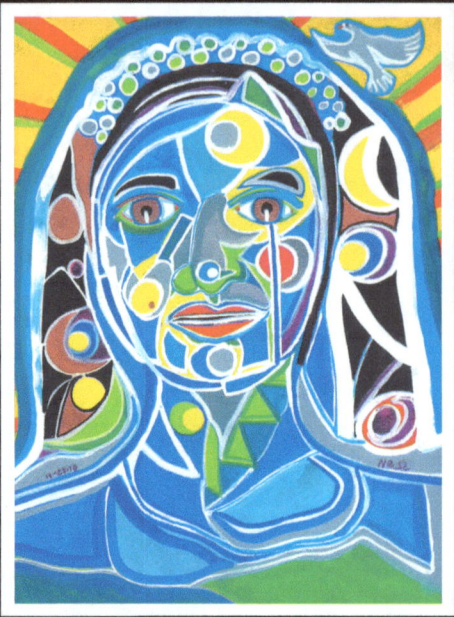
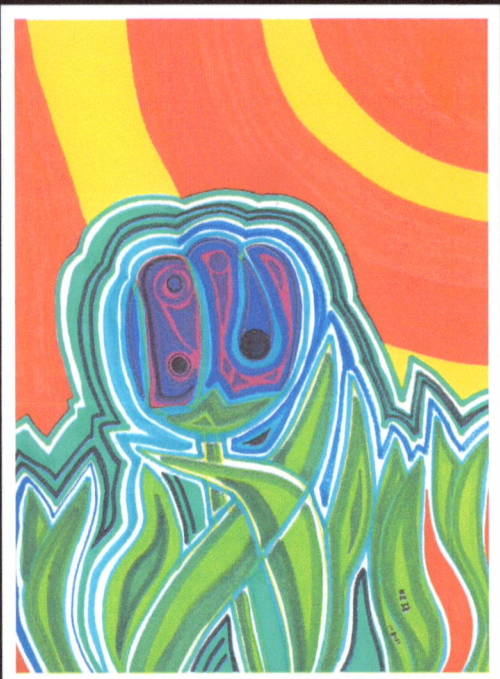
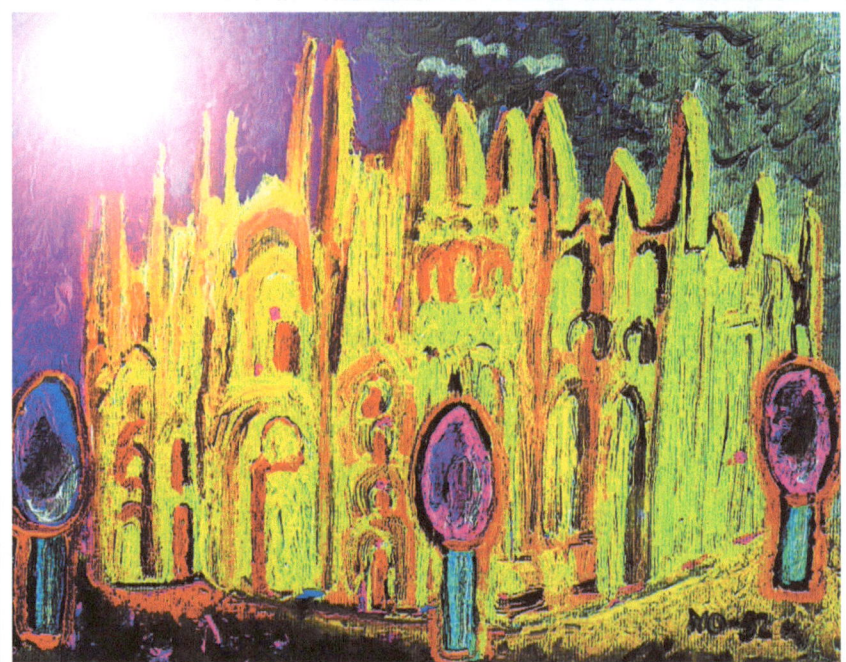

Shirts and paintings and more available at
www.darkono.52.com

www.ingramcontent.com/pod-product-compliance
Lightning Source LLC
Chambersburg PA
CBHW050430180526

45159CB00005B/2483